The Complete Guitar Player Songbook 2

Use with
The Complete Guitar Player course
or on its own!

This songbook is designed to complement
The Complete Guitar Player Book 2, presenting the songs
from the book with full melodic lines and lyrics.
In addition to the songs featured in the series, this book
contains some suitable additional songs to help
you develop your technique and expand your repertoire.

Sometimes, capo and tuning indications are shown.
This is so that you can play along with the original recording
in the right key. If you're playing on your own,
you don't need to worry about these instructions.

WISE PUBLICATIONS

part of The Music Sales Group

London / New York / Paris / Sydney / Copenhagen / Berlin / Madrid / Hong Kong / Tokyo

Published by
WISE PUBLICATIONS
14-15 Berners Street, London W1T 3LJ,
United Kingdom.

Exclusive Distributors:
MUSIC SALES LIMITED
Distribution Centre, Newmarket Road, Bury St Edmunds,
Suffolk IP33 3YB, United Kingdom.
MUSIC SALES PTY LIMITED
Units 3-4, 17 Willfox Street, Condell Park, NSW 2200, Australia.

Order No. AM995423
ISBN 978-1-84772-733-6
This book © Copyright 2014 Wise Publications,
a division of Music Sales Limited.

Edited by Toby Knowles.
Music arranged by Matt Cowe.
Music processed by Paul Ewers Music Design.
Cover designed by Michael Bell Design.
All photographs courtesy of Getty Images:
Johnny Cash, Patsy Cline, Ralph McTell, Van Morrison, Dolly Parton,
Elvis Presley, Simon & Garfunkel, Rod Stewart by Michael Ochs Archives.
The Beatles by John Pratt/Keystone. Newton Faulkner by Caitlin Mogridge/Redferns.
Printed in the EU.

Your Guarantee of Quality
As publishers, we strive to produce every book to the highest commercial standards.
This book has been carefully designed to minimise awkward page turns and to make playing from it a real pleasure.
Particular care has been given to specifying acid-free, neutral-sized paper made from
pulps which have not been elemental chlorine bleached.
This pulp is from farmed sustainable forests and was produced with special regard for the environment.
Throughout, the printing and binding have been planned to ensure a sturdy,
attractive publication which should give years of enjoyment.
If your copy fails to meet our high standards, please inform us and we will gladly replace it.

www.musicsales.com

Brown Eyed Girl

Words & Music by Van Morrison

Strumming style:

Try to memorise the chord sequence. That way, you can concentrate on the sound, rather than reading, when you play this song.

Accompaniment: 4/4 Rhythm

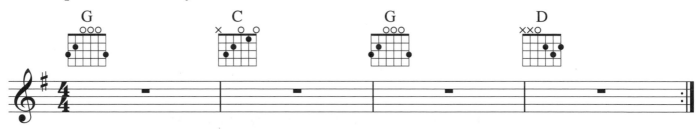

Verse

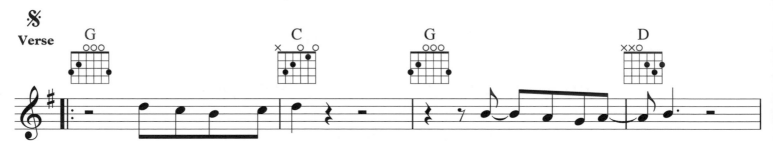

1. Hey where did we go,   days__ when the rains__ came?
2. What - ev - er hap-pened   to Tues-day and so_____ slow?
3. So hard to find my way   now__ that I'm all on my own.

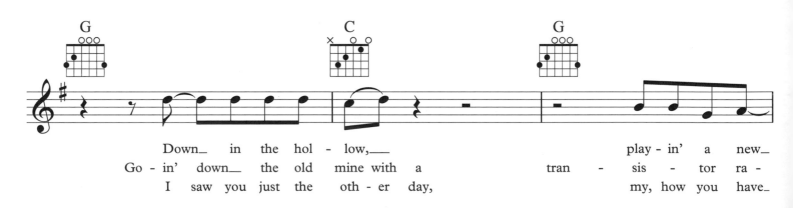

Down__ in the hol - low,__   play - in' a new__
Go - in' down__ the old mine with a   tran - sis - tor ra -
I saw you just the oth - er day,   my, how you have__

__ game.   Laugh - in' and a - run - nin',   hey,__ hey,
-di - o.   Stand - in' in the sun - light laugh - in',
__ grown.   Cast my mem - 'ry back there, Lord,_____

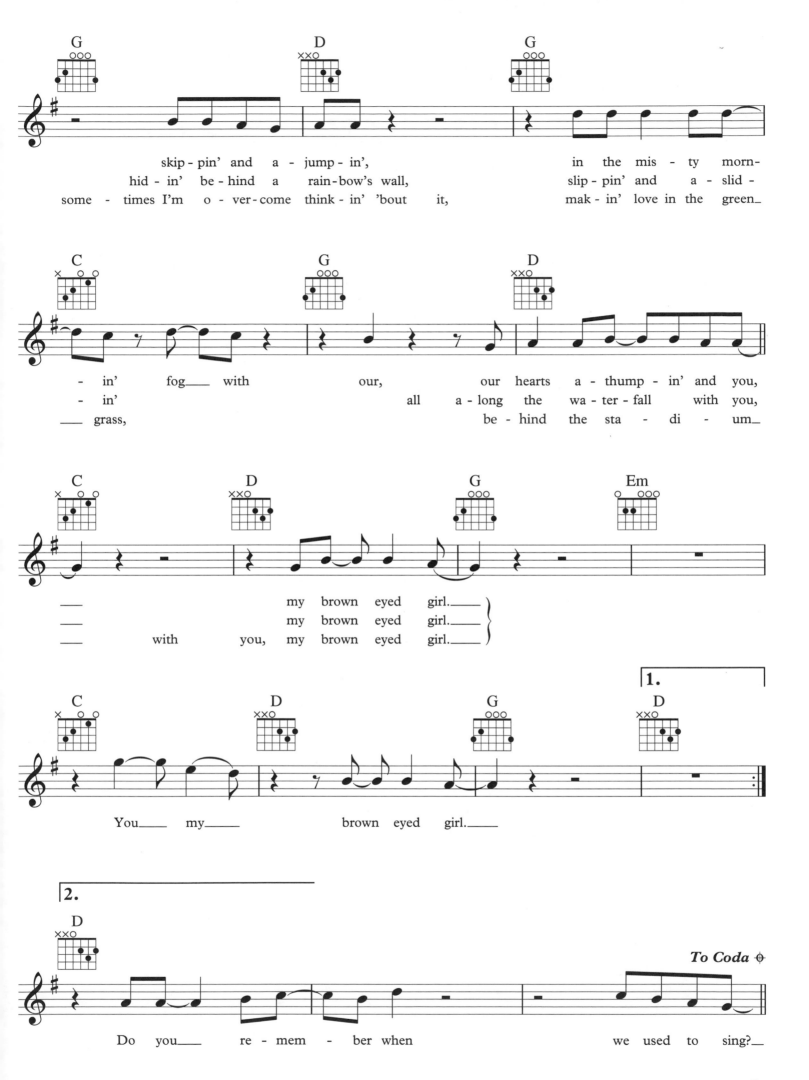

skip - pin' and a - jump - in',   in the mis - ty morn-
hid - in' be - hind a rain-bow's wall,   slip - pin' and a - slid -
some - times I'm o - ver-come think - in' 'bout it,   mak - in' love in the green_

- in' fog___ with   our,   our hearts a - thump - in' and you,
- in'   all a - long the wa - ter - fall with you,
___ grass,   be - hind the sta - di - um_

___   my brown eyed girl.___
___   my brown eyed girl.___
___ with you, my brown eyed girl.___

1.

You___ my___ brown eyed girl.___

2.

To Coda ⊕

Do you___ re - mem - ber when   we used to sing?___

5

Chorus

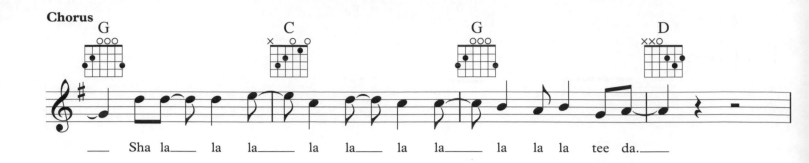

Sha la la la la la la la la la la tee da.

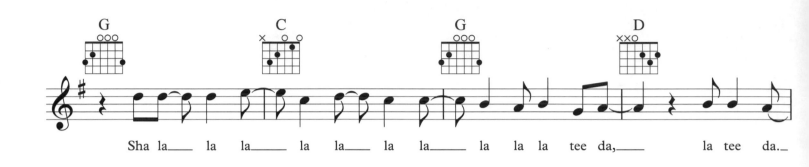

Sha la la la la la la la la la la tee da, la tee da.

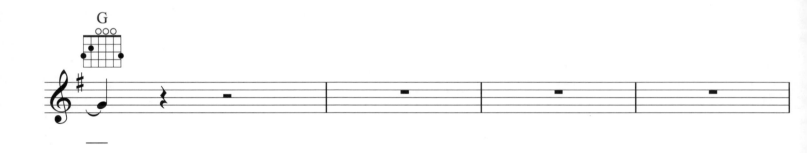

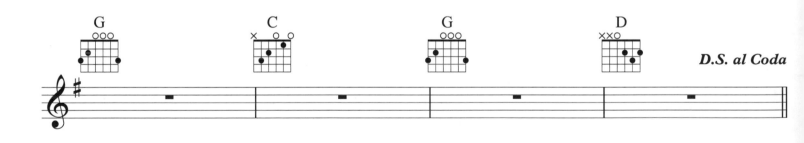

D.S. al Coda

Repeat ad lib. to fade

Coda

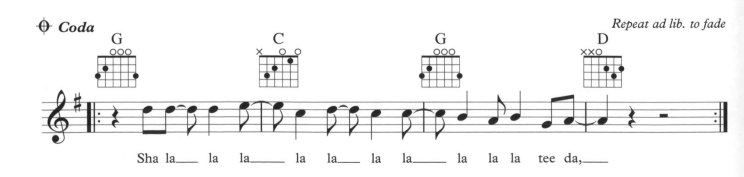

Sha la la la la la la la la la la tee da,

Jolene

Words & Music by Dolly Parton

Arpeggio style:

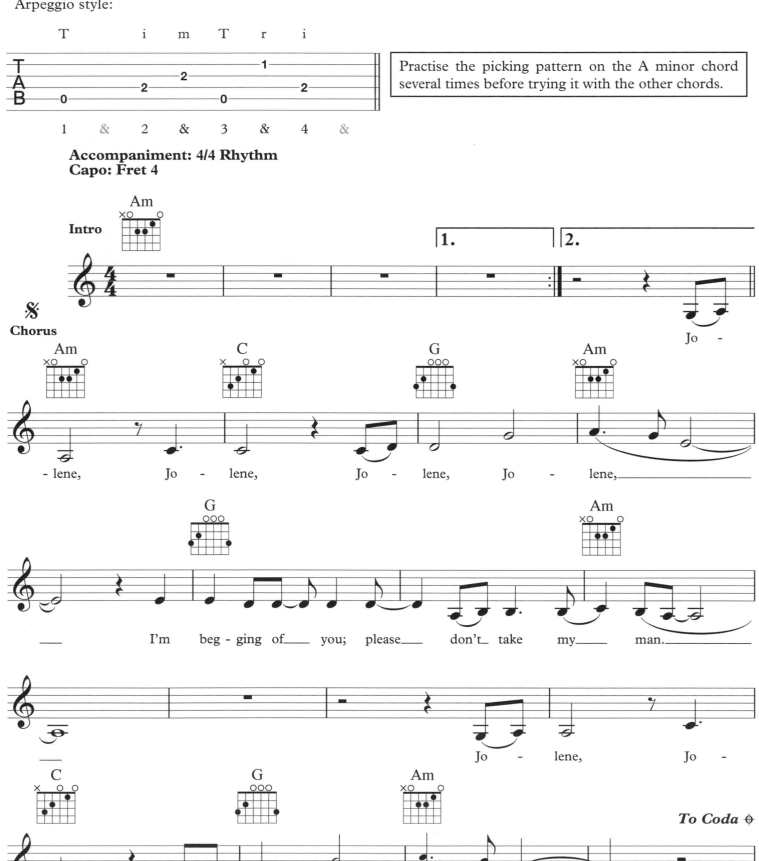

Practise the picking pattern on the A minor chord several times before trying it with the other chords.

Accompaniment: 4/4 Rhythm
Capo: Fret 4

please don't take him just be-cause___ you___ can.___

1. Your___

Verse

Am   C   G

(1.) beau - ty is___ be - yond___ com - pare,___ with flam - ing locks___ of au -
(2.) talks a - bout___ you in___ his sleep, and there's no - thing I___ can do___
3. You could have___ your choice___ of men,___ but I could nev - er love___

Am   G

- burn hair,___ with iv - 'ry skin___ and eyes of em - 'rald___
___ to keep___ from cry - ing when___ he calls your name, Jo -
___ a - gain.___ He's the on - ly one for me, Jo -

Am

___ green.___
- lene.___
- lene.___

Your
And
I

C   G

smile is like a breath___ of spring,___ your voice___ is soft___ like
I can eas - 'ly un - der - stand___ how you___ could eas - 'ly
had to have this talk___ with you,___ my hap - pi - ness___ de -

8

Jackson

Words & Music by Jerry Leiber & Billy Edd Wheeler

Strumming style:

Make a note of the way the thumb picking alternates within the picking pattern for each new chord.

Accompaniment: 4/4 Rhythm

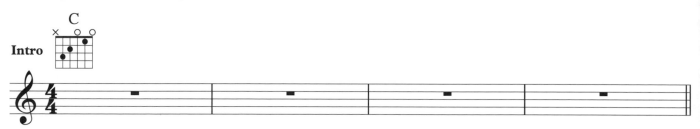

Intro

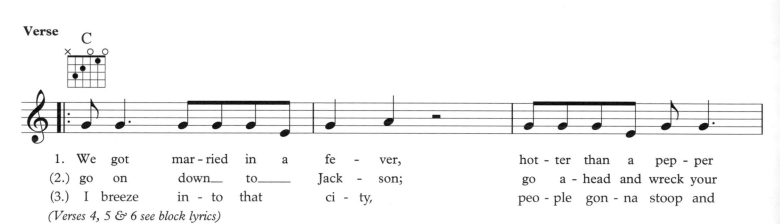

Verse

1. We got mar-ried in a fe-ver,   hot-ter than a pep-per
(2.) go on down to Jack-son;   go a-head and wreck your
(3.) I breeze in-to that ci-ty,   peo-ple gon-na stoop and
(Verses 4, 5 & 6 see block lyrics)

sprout,   we've been talk-in' 'bout Jack-son,
health.   Go play your hand you big-talk-in' man, make a
bow.   (Hah!) All them wo-men gon-na make me,

e-ver since the fire went out.   I'm go-in' to Jack-son,
big fool of your-self.   Yeah, go to Jack-son;
teach 'em what they don't know how.   I'm go-in' to Jack-son,

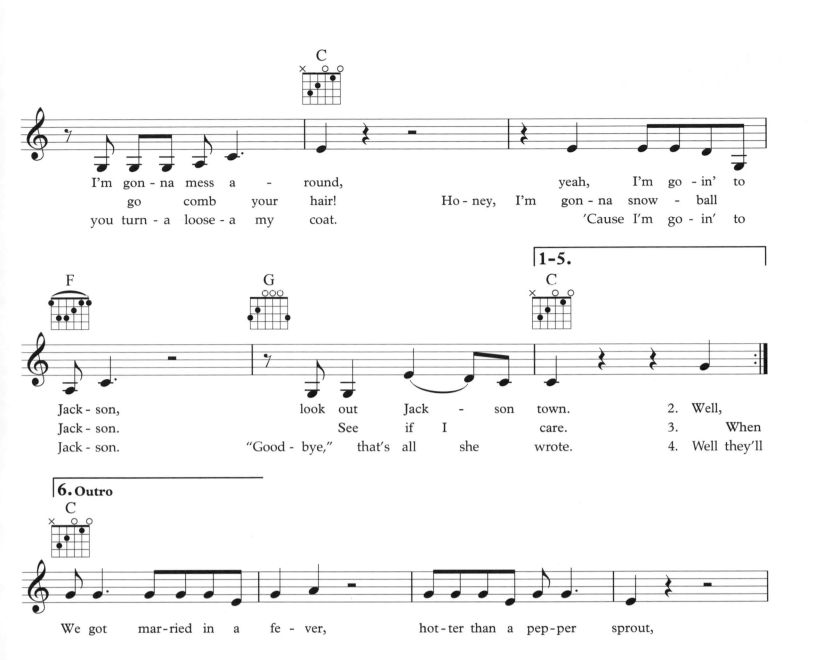

I'm gon-na mess a - round, yeah, I'm go - in' to
go comb your hair! Ho - ney, I'm gon - na snow - ball
you turn - a loose - a my coat. 'Cause I'm go - in' to

1-5.

Jack - son, look out Jack - son town. 2. Well,
Jack - son. See if I care. 3. When
Jack - son. "Good - bye," that's all she wrote. 4. Well they'll

6. Outro

We got mar-ried in a fe - ver, hot-ter than a pep-per sprout,

Fade

we've been talk- in' 'bout Jack-son, e - ver since the fire___ went___ out. I'm go -in' to

Verse 4:
Well they'll laugh at you in Jackson,
And I'll be dancin' on a Pony Keg.
They'll lead you 'round town like a scalded hound,
With your tail tucked between your legs,
Yeah, go to Jackson, you big-talkin' man.
And I'll be waitin' in Jackson, behind my Jay-pan Fan,

Verse 5:
Well now, we got married in a fever,
Hotter than a pepper sprout,
We've been talkin' 'bout Jackson, ever since the fire went.
I'm goin' to Jackson, and that's a fact.
Yeah, we're goin' to Jackson, ain't never comin' back.

11

Yellow Submarine

Words & Music by John Lennon & Paul McCartney

Strumming styles:

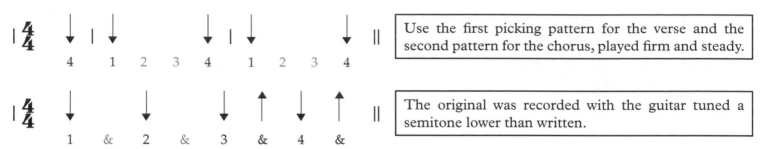

Use the first picking pattern for the verse and the second pattern for the chorus, played firm and steady.

The original was recorded with the guitar tuned a semitone lower than written.

Accompaniment: 4/4 Rhythm (Swing)

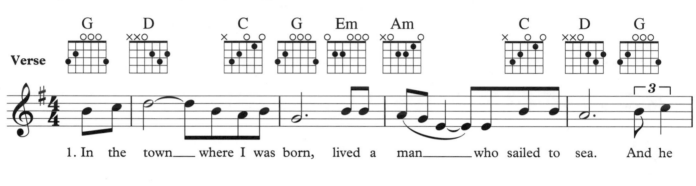

Verse

1. In the town where I was born, lived a man who sailed to sea. And he

told us of his life in the land of sub-mar-ines. So we

sailed on to the sun, till we found the sea of green, and we

lived be-neath the waves in our yel-low sub-mar-ine.

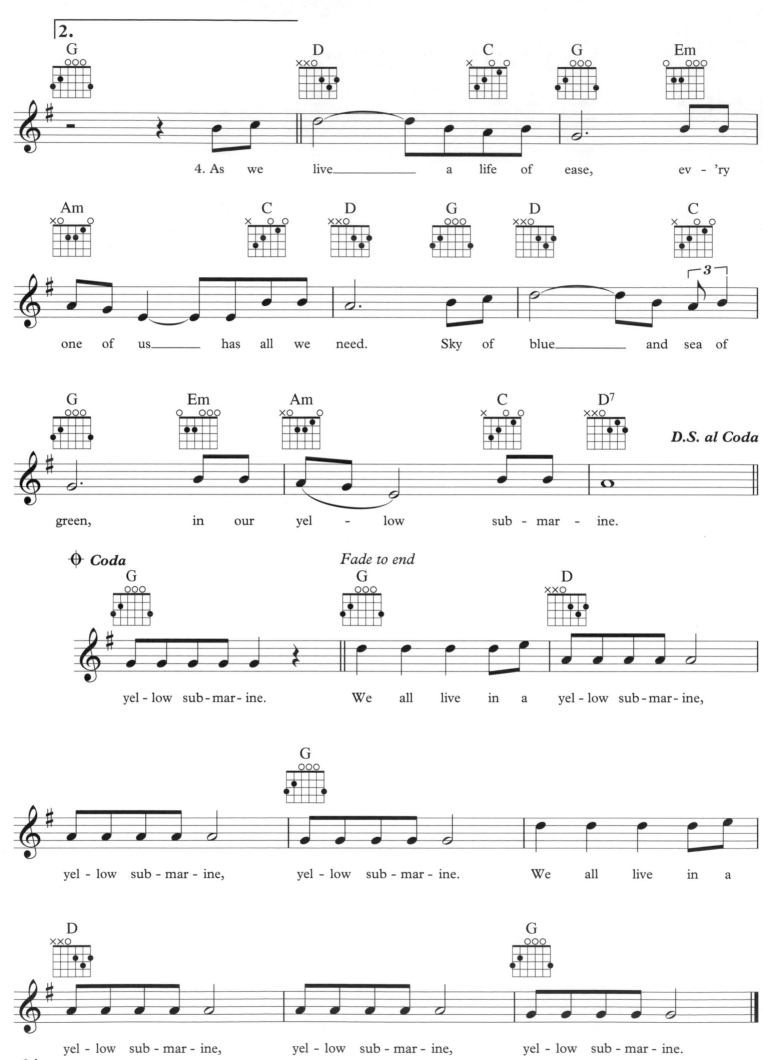

4. As we live_____ a life of ease, ev - 'ry

one of us_____ has all we need. Sky of blue_____ and sea of

D.S. al Coda

green, in our yel - low sub - mar - ine.

Coda

Fade to end

yel - low sub - mar - ine. We all live in a yel - low sub - mar - ine,

yel - low sub - mar - ine, yel - low sub - mar - ine. We all live in a

yel - low sub - mar - ine, yel - low sub - mar - ine, yel - low sub - mar - ine.

Like A Rolling Stone

Words & Music by Bob Dylan

Strumming style:

> Try playing the strumming pattern slowly to begin with, until you can play it smoothly and naturally.

Accompanment: 4/4 Rhythm

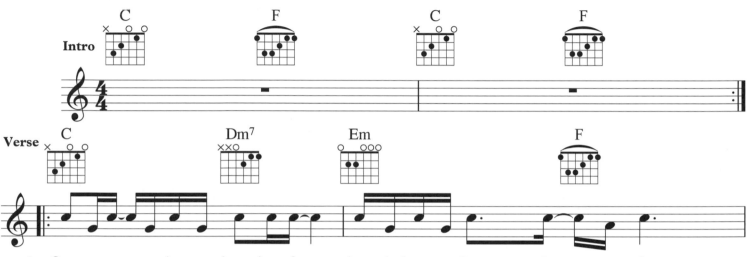

1. Once up-on__ a time you dressed so fine,__ threw the bums a dime in__ your prime,
(2.)__ gone__ to the fi - nest school all right,__ Miss__ Lone-ly, but you know you on-ly used to get

(Verses 3 & 4 see block lyrics)

did - n't you?
juiced in it.__ No -

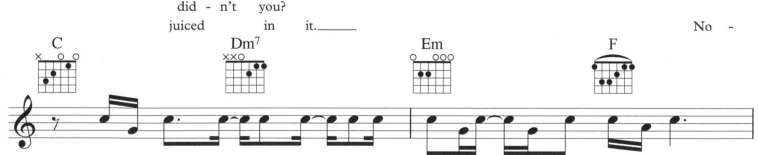

Peo-ple called, said "Be - ware,__ doll, you're bound to fall,"__ you thought they were all
-bo-dy's ev - er taught you how__ to live out__ on the street, and now you're gon - na have to get

a kid - ding you
used to it.__

You used___ to laugh a - bout
You say you nev - er com - pro - mise___

ev - 'ry - bo - dy that was hang - ing out.___
with a mys - te - ry tramp, but now you re - al - ize_____

Now you don't___ talk so loud,
he's not sell - ing a - ny a - li - bis,_____

now you don't seem so proud a - bout___ hav - ing to be scroung - ing___
as you stare in-to the va - cuum of his eyes and say "Do you want to

your next meal._____
make a deal?"_____ How does it feel?___

Chorus

How does it feel_____

16 —

to be on your own,____

to be with-out a home,__
with no di-rec-tion____ home,__

____

like a com-plete__ un-known,
a com-plete__ un-known,____

like a roll-ing stone?____

1-3.

4.

2. Oh, you've
3. Oh, you've
4. Oh,____

Verse 3:
Oh, you've never turned around to see the frowns on the
Jugglers and the clowns when they all did tricks for you
Never understood that it ain't no good
You shouldn't let other people get your kicks for you
You used to ride on the chrome horse with your diplomat
Who carried on his shoulder a Siamese cat
Ain't it hard when you discover that he really wasn't where it's at
After he took from you everything he could steal?

Verse 4:
Oh, Princess on the steeple and all the pretty people they all
Drinking, thinking that they got it made
Exchanging all precious gifts
But you better take a diamond ring
You better pawn it, babe
You used to be so amused
At Napoleon in rags and the language that he used
Go to him now, he calls you, you can't refuse
When you ain't got nothing, you got nothing to lose
You're invisible now you've got no secrets to conceal.

Sailing

Words & Music by Gavin Sutherland

Arpeggio style:

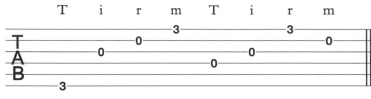

| The individual notes of the picking pattern should run smoothly into each other to create a flowing line. |

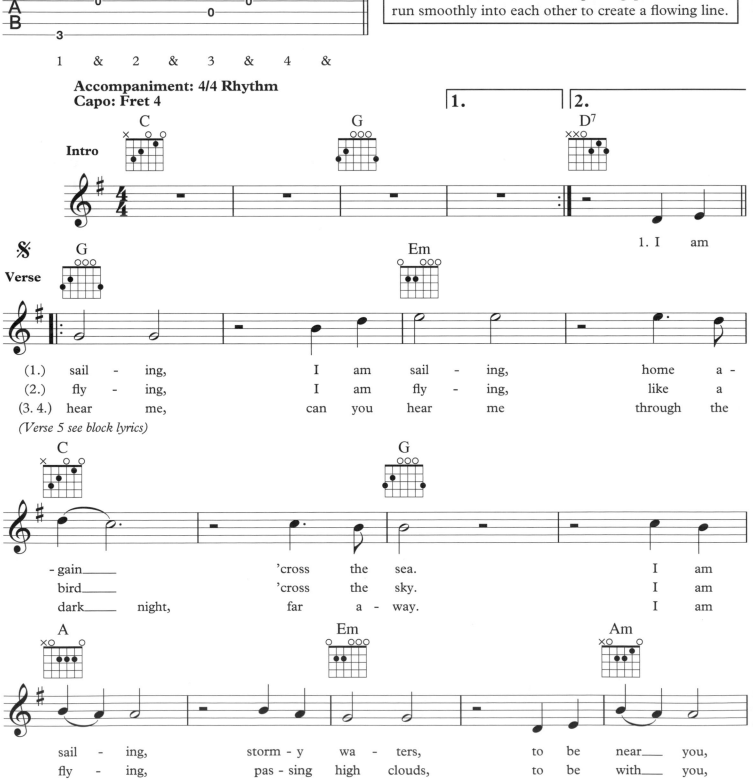

Verse 5:
We are sailing, we are sailing,
Home again 'cross the sea.
We are sailing stormy waters,
To be near you, to be free.

Mrs. Robinson

Words & Music by Paul Simon

Play the picked riff wherever you see the chord of **E**, or else use the strumming pattern throughout.

Arpeggio style:

Strumming style:

Accompaniment: 4/4 Rhythm
Capo: Fret 2

Intro

De de de de de de de de de de de de de de.____

Do do do do do do do do do.____

De de de de de de de de de____ de de de de de.____

And here's to you____

20

Chorus

1. 2. ___ Mis-sus Ro - bin - son, ___ Je - sus loves_ you more ___ than you ___ will know, ___
3. (%) ___ Joe Di Mag - gi - o? ___ A na - tion turns it's lone - ly eyes to you. ___

___ whoa,_ whoa, whoa. ___ God bless you please, ___
___ Ooh,_ ooh, ooh. ___ What's that you say ___

___ Mis - sus Ro - bin - son, ___ Hea - ven holds a place ___ for those_ who pray. ___
___ Mis - sus. Ro - bin - son, ___ Jol - ting Joe ___ has left ___ and gone_ a - way. ___

To Coda ⊕

___ Hey,_ hey, hey. ___ Hey,_ hey, hey. ___
___ Hey,_ hey. hey. ___ Hey,_ hey, hey. ___

___
___

1. We'd

Verse

like to know_ a lit - tle bit a - bout ___ you for ___ our files. ___
2. Hide it in a hid - ing place_ where no ___ one e - ver goes, ___
3. Sit - ting on a so - fa on ___ a Sun - day af - ter - noon, ___

We'd like to help___ you
put it in your pan-
go - ing to the can-

learn   to help your - self.   Look a-round you, all___
- try   with___ your   cup___ cakes.   It's a lit - tle se-
- di - dates_ de - bate.___   Laugh a - bout   it,

___ you need___ are   sym - pa - the - tic eyes._____
- cret,   just___ the   Ro - bin - son's___   af - fair,_____
shout a - bout___   it   when you've   got   to   choose,___

Stroll   a - round___   the   grounds   un -
most   of   all_____   you've   got   to   hide_
ev - 'ry   way   you   look   at   this___   you   lose.

1, 2.   **3.**   *D.S. al Coda*

- til   you   feel   at   home.___   And   here's   to   you___   Where   have   you   gone___
___   it   from   the   kids.___   Koo   koo   ka - choo___

⊕ Coda   E

Repeat ad lib. to fade

22

Dream Catch Me

Words & Music by Crispin Hunt, Newton Faulkner & Gordon Mills

There's a place I go____ when I'm a - lone,____ do an-y-thing I want,____ be an-y-one I wan - na be, but it is us____ I see____ and I____ can - not____ be - lieve____ I'm fall - in'. That's where I'm go - in', where are you go - in'?_____ Hold it close;___won't let__ this go.____ Dream catch__ me,____ yeah.____ Dream catch____ me when I fall,_____

1. or else I won't come back at all.__ _____

2. or else I won't come back at all.__

Girl From The North Country

Words & Music by Bob Dylan

Arpeggio style:

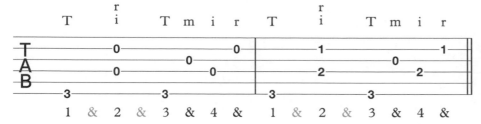

C/G is just a embellishment of G: try playing the song through, adding C/G when you've got the hang of the picking pattern.

Accompaniment: 4/4/ Rhythm
Capo: Fret 3

1. If you're trav - 'lin' in the north coun - try fair.
2. If you go____ when____ snow - flakes____ storm,
3. Please____ see____ if her hair hangs____ long,

(Verses 4 & 6 see block lyrics)
(Verses 5 Instrumental)

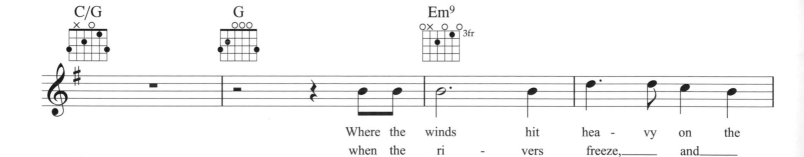

Where the winds hit hea - vy on the
when the ri - vers freeze,____ and____
If it rolls and falls____ all____

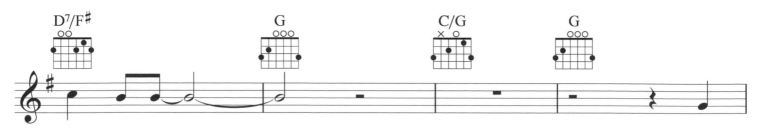

bor - der - line.____   Re -
sum - mer ends.____
down her breast.____

Fairytale Of New York

Words & Music by Shane MacGowan & Jem Finer

Arpeggio style:

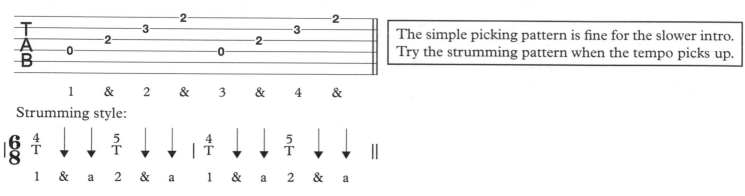

The simple picking pattern is fine for the slower intro.
Try the strumming pattern when the tempo picks up.

Strumming style:

Accompaniment: 4/4 Rhythm - Slowly

Intro

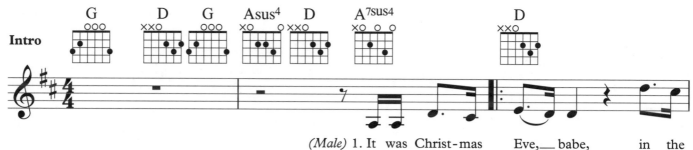

(Male) 1. It was Christ-mas Eve,__ babe, in the
luck - y one, came in

drunk tank, when an old man said to me,__ "Won't see an-oth-er one".__ And then he
eight - een to one, I've got a____ feel-ing____ this year's for me and you.__ So Hap-py

sang a song, "The rare old moun-tain dew". I turned my face a-way,__ and dreamed a-
Christ - mas; I love you, ba - by. I can see a bet-ter time,__ when all our

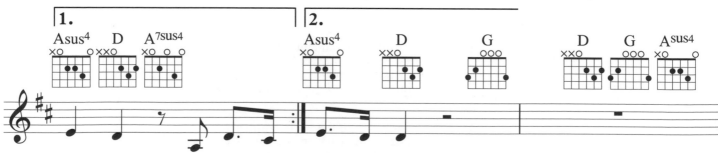

1.

- bout you. 2. Got on a

2.

dreams come true.

28

Accompaniment: 6/8 Rhythm - Faster

3. *(Female)* They got cars big as bars, they got riv - ers of gold; but the wind goes right through you, it's no place for the old.___ When you first took my hand on a cold___ Christ - mas Eve, you pro - mised me Broad - way was wait - ing for me.___ 4. You were hand - some. *(M)* You were pret - ty, Queen of New York Ci - ty. *(Both)* When the

(5.) bum,___ you're a punk! *(M)* You're an old slut on junk,___ ly - ing

band fin - ished play - ing, they howled out for more.___ Sin -

there al - most dead on a drip on that bed!___ *(F)* You

29

Instrumental

5. *(Female)* You're a

6. *(Male)* I_____ could have been some-one.___ *(F)* Well, so could an-y-one.___ You took my dreams___ ___ from me when I first found_ you.___ *(M)* I kept them with me, babe;_ I put them with my own.___ Can't_ make it all a-lone;_ I've built_ my dreams a-round you. The

31

boys   of the N.   Y.   P.   D.   choir___   still   sing-ing___   "Gal - way

Bay".   And   the   bells___   are   ring-ing   out___   for   Christ-mas   Day.___

(Strings)

Repeat to fade

32

Fields Of Gold

Words & Music by Sting

Strumming style:

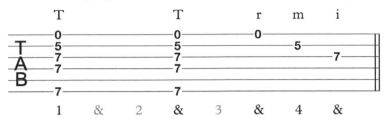

Accompaniment: 4/4 Rhythm

Verse 1: You'll re-mem-ber me when the west wind moves up-on the fields of bar-ley. You'll for-get the sun in his jeal-ous sky as we walk in fields of gold.

Verse 2: stay with me, will you be my love a-mong the fields of bar-ley? We'll for-get the sun in his jeal-ous sky as we lie in fields of gold.

So she took her love for to gaze a-while up-

See the west wind move like a lov-er so up-

-on the fields___ of bar - ley. In his arms she fell as her
-on the fields___ of bar - ley. Feel her bo - dy rise when you

hair came down a - mong___ the fields_ of gold.
kiss her mouth a - mong___ the fields_ of gold.

Will you

Middle

I nev-er made pro-mi-ses light - ly and there have been some that I've bro - ken,

but I swear_ in the days still left we'll walk___ in fields_ of gold.

We'll___ walk in fields_ of gold.

Instrumental

American Pie

Words & Music by Don McLean

Strumming style:

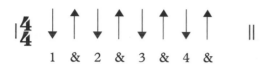

1 & 2 & 3 & 4 &

> This is a long song, but the structure's pretty simple.
> Memorising the repeating sections will make it easier.

Accompaniment: 4/4 Rhythm Freely

Verse

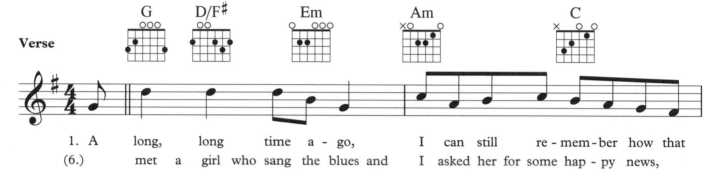

1. A long, long time a-go, I can still re-mem-ber how that
(6.) met a girl who sang the blues and I asked her for some hap-py news,

mu-sic used to make me smile.___ And I I knew if I had my chance, that
she just smiled and turned a-way. I went down to the sa-cred store where

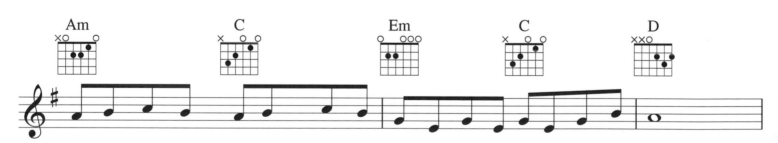

I could make those peo-ple dance and may-be they'd be hap-py for a while.
I'd heard the mu-sic years be-fore, But the man there said the mu-sic would-n't play. And

But Feb-ru-a-ry made___ me shi-ver with ev-'ry pa-per I'd
in the streets the chil-dren screamed, the lo-vers cried and the

So }

A   D⁷

___ how to dance___   real   slow?_____   Well, I
___   from___ you and me.   Oh and
- delines   in a cast.   Now the

Em   D   Em

know that you're___ in   love with him___ 'cos I   saw   you   danc - in'
while the King___ was   look - ing   down   the   jes - ter stole his
half - time air___ was   sweet per - fume   while   ser - geants played a

D   C   G/B   Am

in   the   gym.___   You both kicked off your shoes_____   man, I
thor - ny crown.   The cour - troom was   ad - journed,_____   no
march - ing tune.___   We   all   got   up   to   dance,_____   oh but we

C   D   G   D/F♯

dig those   rhy - thm 'n' blues.___   I was a lone - ly teen - age
ver - dict was   re - turned.   And while Len - non   read   a book
ne - ver got   the   chance.   'cause the pla - yers tried to

Em   Am   C

bronc - in' buck   with a pink car - na - tion and a   pick - up truck___   but I
___ on Marx,   the quar - tet prac - ticed   in   the park,   and
take the field,   the mar - ching band___   re - fused to yield.___

G   D/F♯   Em

knew I_____   was   out   of luck   the day___
___ we sang   dir - ges   in   the dark   the day___
Do you re - call_____   what was   re - vealed.   the day___

39

the mu - - sic died.
the mu - - sic died.
the mu - - sic died.

1, 2, 3. | **4.**

I start - ed sing - ing, He was sing - ing
We____ were sing - ing,
We start - ed sing - ing,

Chorus

bye, bye Miss Am - er - i - can Pie. Drove my Che - vy to the le - vee but the

le - vee was dry.____ Them good old boys____ were drink - ing

whis - key and rye,____ sing - in' this - 'll be the day that I die,

D.C. al Coda

this - 'll be the day that I die.

I

Verse 5:
And there we were all in one place,
A generation lost in space
With no time left to start again.
So come on, Jack be nimble, Jack be quick
Jack flash sat on a candlestick
Cause fire is the devil's only friend.

And as I watched him on the stage
My hands were clenched in fists of rage
No angel born in hell
Could break that Satan's spell.

And as the flames climbed high into the night
To light the sacrificial rite,
I saw Satan laughing with delight
The day the music died.
He was singing ...

Chorus

Can't Help Falling In Love

Words & Music by George David Weiss, Hugo Peretti & Luigi Creatore

Strumming style:

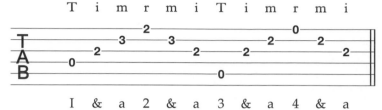

Count the rhythm in four beats, with each beat split into three parts: it'll make it easier to keep time.

Accompaniment: 12/8 Rhythm

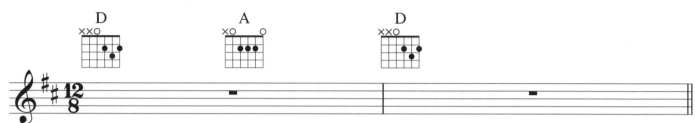

Verse

Eternal Flame

Words & Music by Susanna Hoffs, Tom Kelly & Billy Steinberg

Strumming style:

1 e & a 2 e & a 3 e & a 4 e & a

> The strumming pattern looks simple enough, but the sixteenths move quite quickly. Try it slowly until you can play the pattern smoothly, then pick up the tempo. Play it with a light and even touch.

Accompaniment: 4/4 Rhythm

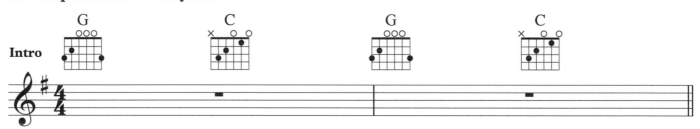

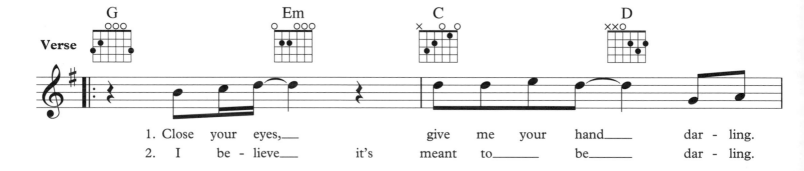

1. Close your eyes,___ give me your hand___ dar - ling.
2. I be - lieve___ it's meant to___ be___ dar - ling.

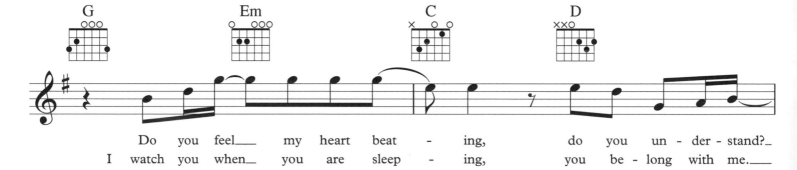

Do you feel___ my heart beat - ing, do you un - der - stand?___
I watch you when___ you are sleep - ing, you be - long with me.___

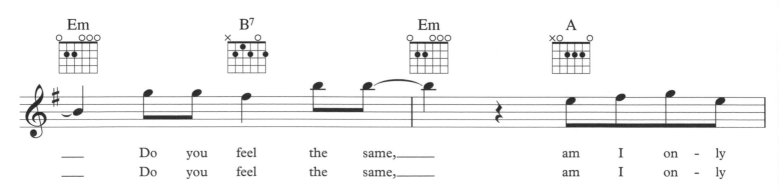

___ Do you feel the same,___ am I on - ly
___ Do you feel the same,___ am I on - ly

Streets Of London

Words & Music by Ralph McTell

Strumming style:

Accompaniment: 4/4 Rhythm
Capo: Fret 4

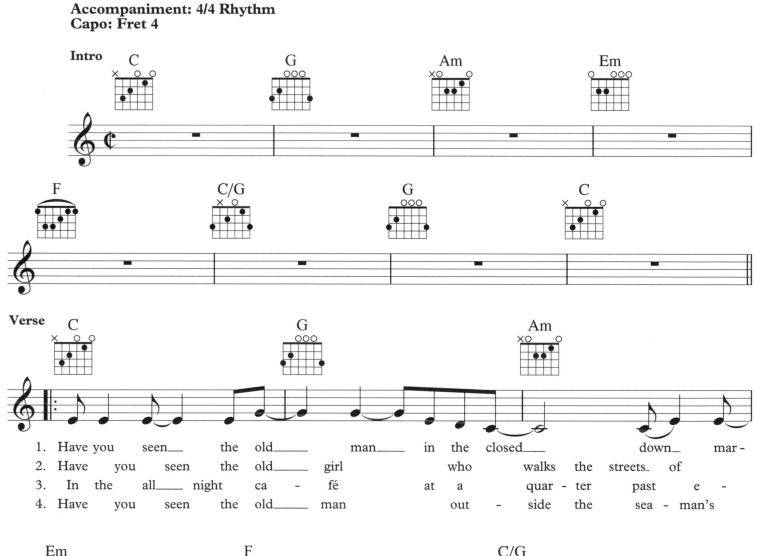

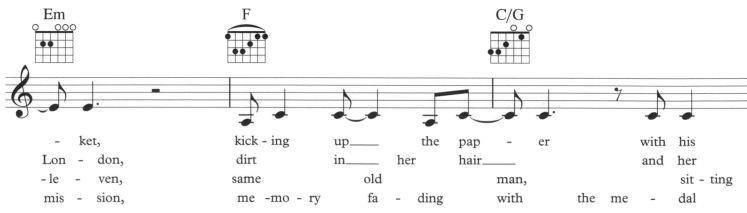

1. Have you seen___ the old___ man___ in the closed___ down__ mar-
2. Have you seen the old___ girl who walks the streets__ of
3. In the all__ night ca - fé at a quar - ter past e -
4. Have you seen the old___ man out - side the sea - man's

- ket, kick - ing up__ the pap - er with his
Lon - don, dirt in__ her hair___ and her
- le - ven, same old man, sit - ting
mis - sion, me - mo - ry fa - ding with the me - dal

Stuck In The Middle With You

Words & Music by Gerry Rafferty & Joe Egan

Strumming style:

(Intro pattern)

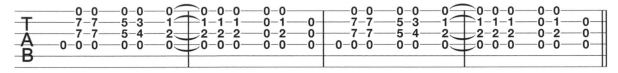

1 & 2 & 3 & 4 &   1 & 2 & 3 & 4 &   1 & 2 & 3 & 4 &   1 & 2 & 3 & 4 &

(✗ = damped strings)

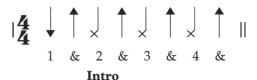

1 & 2 & 3 & 4 &

Try the tabbed strumming pattern for the intro with the chords shown (above), or else play the second pattern (left) throughout.

Intro

Accompaniment: 4/4 Rhythm

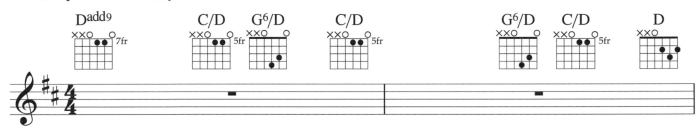

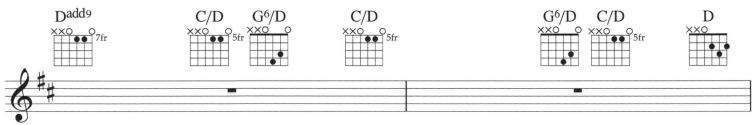

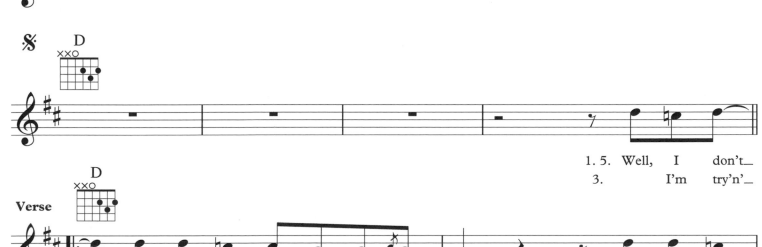

1. 5. Well, I don't__
3. I'm try'n'__

Verse

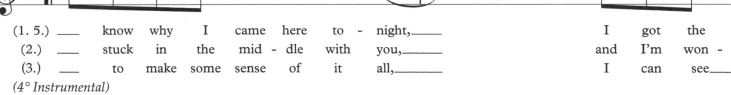

(1. 5.) __ know why I came here to - night,_____   I got the
(2.) __ stuck in the mid - dle with you,_____   and I'm won -
(3.) __ to make some sense of it all,_____   I can see__

(4° Instrumental)

49

feel - ing that some - thing ain't right,_____ I'm so scared_
- d'ring what it is I should do._____ It's so hard_
___ that it makes no sense at all._____ Is it cool_

G

___ in case I fall off my chair,_____ and I'm wond-
___ to keep the smile from my face,_____ Los - ing con -
___ to go to sleep on the floor?_____ I don't think_

D

- 'ring how I'll get down those stairs._____
-trol, yeah, I'm all ov - er the place._____ } Clowns_
___ that I can take an - y - more._____ }

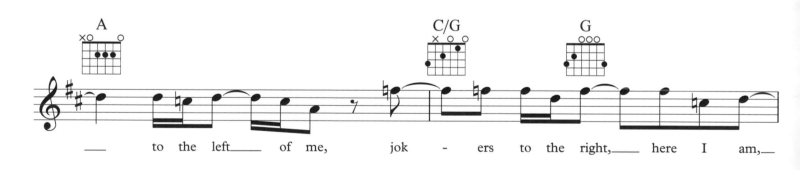

A   C/G   G

___ to the left_____ of me, jok - ers to the right,_____ here I am,_

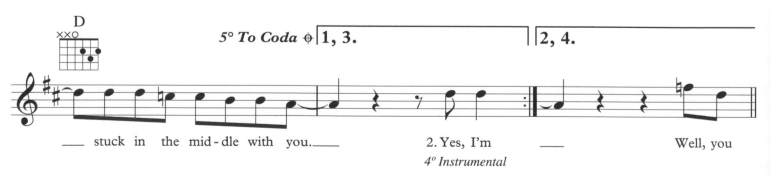

D

5° To Coda ⊕ | 1, 3. | 2, 4.

___ stuck in the mid - dle with you._____ 2. Yes, I'm ___ Well, you

4° Instrumental

50

start-ed out with no-thing and you're proud that you're a self-made man.

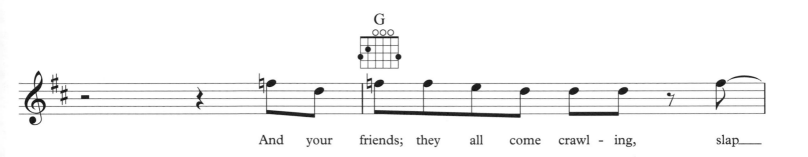

And your friends; they all come crawl-ing, slap

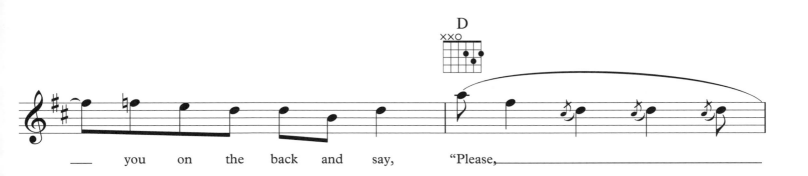

you on the back and say, "Please,

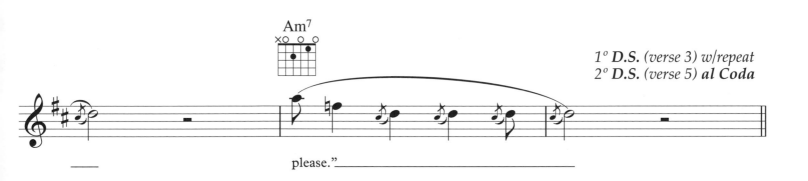

*1° **D.S.** (verse 3) w/repeat*
*2° **D.S.** (verse 5) **al Coda***

please."

Yes, I'm stuck in the mid-dle with you. Here I am

Crazy

Words & Music by Willie Nelson

Strumming style:

Play this pattern in a lazy, unhurried fashion, accenting the first and third beats with a thumb-picked bass note.

Accompaniment: 12/8 Rhythm
Capo: Fret 1

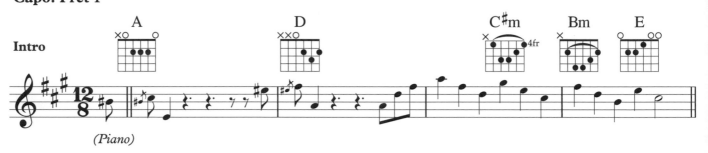

(Piano)

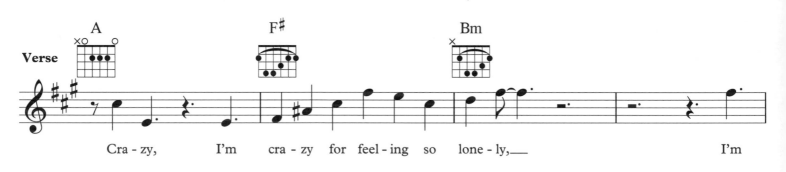

Cra - zy, I'm cra - zy for feel - ing so lone - ly,___ I'm

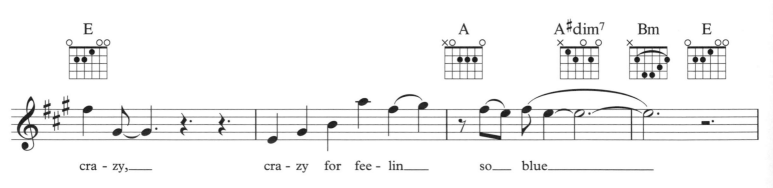

cra - zy,___ cra - zy for fee - lin___ so___ blue_____

I knew you'd love me as long as you want - ed,___ and then

some day___ you'd leave me for some-bo-dy new.

Wor - ry,___ why do I let my-self wor - ry?___

Won - d'rin'___ what in the world did I do?_____ Oh,

cra - zy___ for think-ing that my love could hold you,___ I'm

To Coda ⊕

cra - zy for try-in' and cra - zy for cry-in' and I'm cra - zy for lov - ing

D.S. al Coda   ⊕ **Coda**

you.   you.

Suspicious Minds

Words & Music by Francis Zambon

Arpeggio styles:

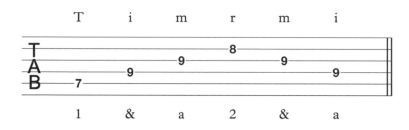

> Use the first picking pattern for the 4/4 rhythm, but the second one for the slower middle section in 6/8.

Accompaniment: 4/4 Rhythm (6/8 Rhythm for Middle)

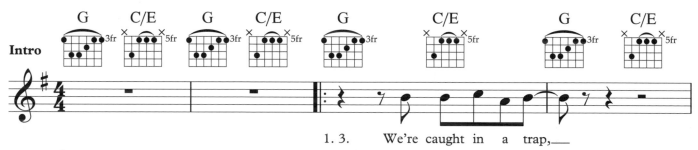

1. 3.   We're caught in a trap,___
2. So if an   old friend I know,___

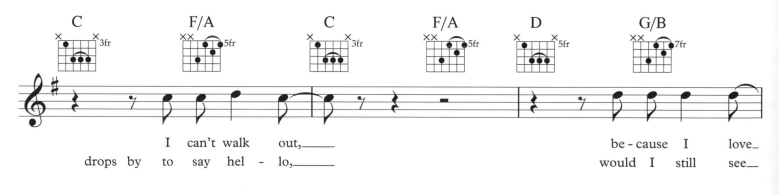

    I can't walk   out,_____   be - cause I   love_
drops by to say hel - lo,_____   would I still   see_

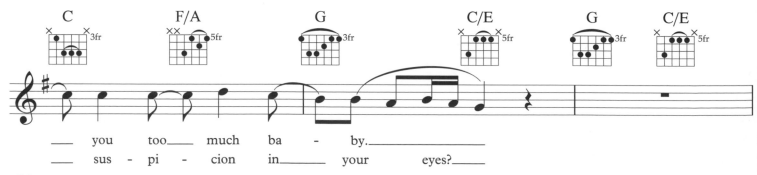

___ you too___ much ba - by.___
___ sus - pi - cion in___ your   eyes?___

To Coda ⊕

Chorus

Slower

Middle

55

Let's don't let a good thing die,_____ when, ho-ney, you know I'll_ nev-er

D.S. al Coda

lie to you.___ Mm._____ Yeah, yeah._____

⊕ *Coda*

when you don't be - lieve___ a word_ I say?_____

Oh, don't you know I'm caught in a trap.____

I can't walk_ out,___ (Ooh.)_____ be - cause_ I love

Repeat to fade

___ you too___ much ba - by._____ Oh, don't you know I'm

1 2 3 4 5 6 7 8 9